INCREDIBLE SPACE

Space Travelers

by Steve Kortenkamp

Reading Consultant:
Barbara J. Fox
Reading Specialist
North Carolina State University

Capstone press®

Mankato, Minnesota

Blazers is published by Capstone Press,
151 Good Counsel Drive, P.O. Box 669, Mankato, Minnesota 56002.
www.capstonepress.com

Library of Congress Cataloging-in-Publication Data
Kortenkamp, Steve.
    Space travelers/by Steve Kortenkamp.
    p. cm. — (Blazers. Incredible space)
    Includes bibliographical references and index.
    Summary: "Discusses the work astronauts do as well as future space explorations to the Moon
and Mars" — Provided by publisher.
    ISBN-13: 978-1-4296-2320-9 (hardcover)
    ISBN-10: 1-4296-2320-9 (hardcover)
    1. Astronautics — Juvenile literature. 2. Outer space — Juvenile literature. I. Title.
TL793.K6632 2009
629.45 — dc22   2008029827

Editorial Credits
Abby Czeskleba, editor; Ted Williams, designer; Jo Miller, photo researcher

Photo Credits
Getty Images Inc./National Geographic/Pierre Mion, 23
NASA, 5, 6, 9, 10, 12, 15, 16–17, 19, 20, 24, 25, 28–29, cover; JPL, 27
Shutterstock/argus (technology background), throughout; hcss5 (minimal code background
    vector), throughout

1 2 3 4 5 6 14 13 12 11 10 09

Table of Contents

chapter 1

Riding a Rocket

Three, two, one . . . blast off! The **space shuttle** lifts off the ground. Seven astronauts leave Earth in the shuttle.

space shuttle

a vehicle that carries astronauts into space and back to Earth

Space shuttle *Atlantis* flies above Earth.

Astronauts **orbit** Earth in space shuttles. They see it as a blue ball floating in space. One day, astronauts will explore distant planets like Mars.

orbit
to travel around an object in space

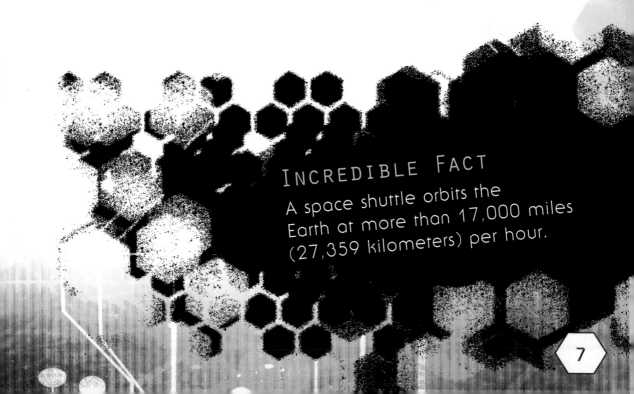

INCREDIBLE FACT
A space shuttle orbits the Earth at more than 17,000 miles (27,359 kilometers) per hour.

chapter 2

Working in Space

Working in space can be hard on an astronaut's body. It feels like there is no **gravity** in space. Human bones and muscles become weak. Astronauts exercise to keep their muscles strong.

gravity

a force that pulls objects together

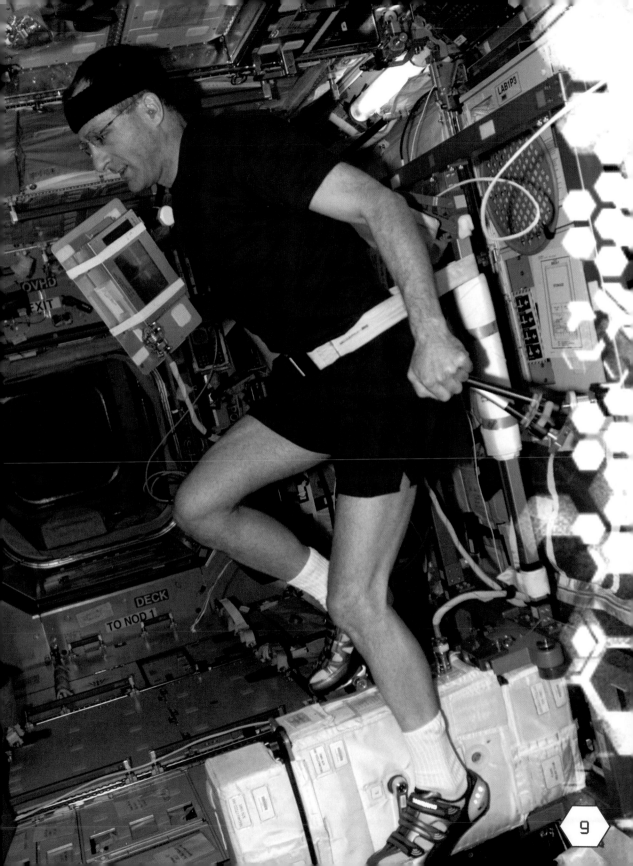

Astronauts have many jobs in space. They do experiments and go on **space walks** to fix equipment. Astronauts are tied to the spacecraft during space walks so they don't float away.

space walk

a period of time when an astronaut leaves the spacecraft to move around in space

Two astronauts add new equipment to the *ISS*.

Astronauts are building the *International Space Station* (*ISS*). Space shuttles carry pieces of the station into orbit. Astronauts attach the pieces to the space station.

International Space Station
a place for astronauts to live and work in space

Astronauts use tools like giant robot arms. The robot arms help astronauts control large space station pieces.

INCREDIBLE FACT
The finished *ISS* will be larger than a soccer field.

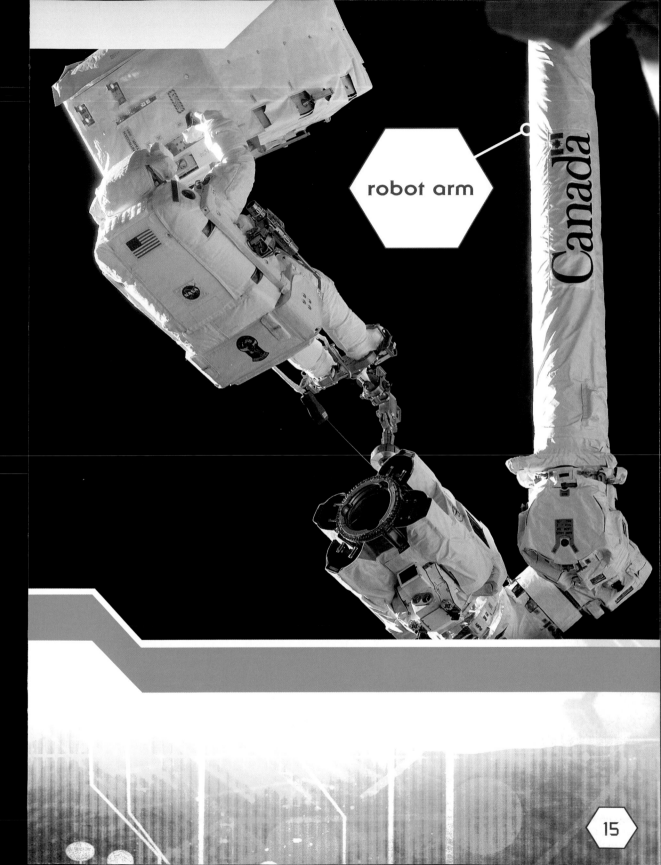

robot arm

Canada

Diagram

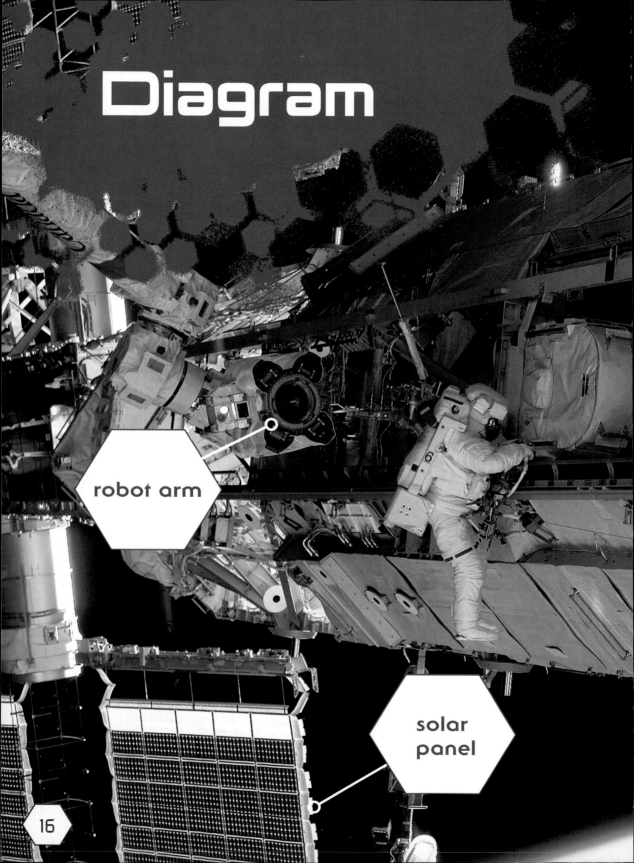

robot arm

solar
panel

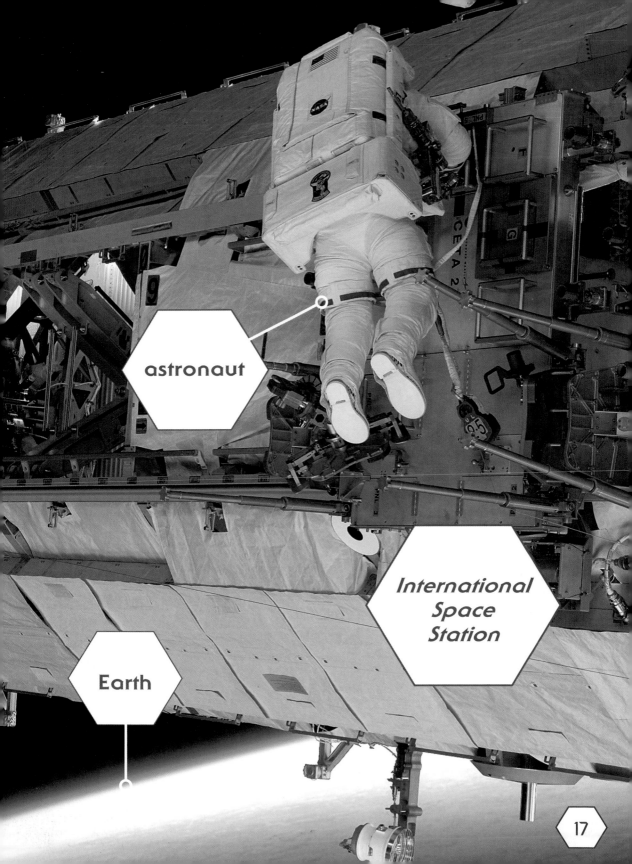

astronaut

International
Space
Station

Earth

chapter 3

Exploring Space

Astronauts may one day live on the Moon. They want to learn more about the Moon. They also want to know why some planets don't have moons.

INCREDIBLE FACT

Mercury and Venus don't have any moons. Jupiter and Saturn each have more than 50 moons.

Astronauts may live in a base on the Moon.
They may also grow plants for food in the base.

Robots will help astronauts explore the Moon. Robots will look for water on the Moon. Astronauts can turn the water into air. Astronauts may also grow plants for food.

robot

a machine people program to do jobs

INCREDIBLE FACT
U.S. astronauts plan to return to the Moon by 2020.

chapter 4

Traveling to Mars

Astronauts will travel more than 150 million miles (241 million kilometers) to reach Mars. The trip to Mars will take about six months.

A new type of space station may one day travel to Mars.

Astronauts may drill holes to search for life on Mars.

Astronauts will be the first people to explore Mars. They will study the planet and search for signs of **Martian** life.

Martian

something on or from the planet Mars

Scientists think Mars was once a wet planet. Today, Mars is like a **desert**. Astronauts want to learn why Mars dried out. They may be able to solve this mystery by exploring Mars.

desert

a dry area with little rain

Robots are studying Mars before astronauts arrive on the planet.

Hello from Space!

Glossary

desert (DE-zuhrt) — a dry area with little rain

equipment (i-KWIP-muhnt) — the machines and tools needed for a job or an activity

experiment (ik-SPEER-uh-muhnt) — a scientific test to find out how something works

gravity (GRAV-uh-tee) — a force that pulls objects together

International Space Station (in-tur-NASH-uh-nuhl SPAYSS STAY-shuhn) — a place for astronauts to live and work in space

Martian (MAHR-shuhn) — something on or from the planet Mars

orbit (OR-bit) — to travel around an object in space

planet (PLAN-it) — a large object that moves around a star

robot (ROH-bot) — a machine people program to do jobs

space shuttle (SPAYSS SHUT-ul) — a vehicle that carries astronauts into space and back to Earth

space walk (SPAYSS WAWK) — a period of time when an astronaut leaves the spacecraft to move around in space

Read More

Flammang, James. *Space Travel.* Innovation in Transportation. Ann Arbor, Mich.: Cherry Lake, 2009.

Grego, Peter. *Exploring the Moon.* QEB Space Guides. North Mankato, Minn.: QEB, 2007.

Kortenkamp, Steve. *Space Tourism.* The Solar System. Mankato, Minn.: Capstone Press, 2008.

Internet Sites

FactHound offers a safe, fun way to find educator-approved Internet sites related to this book.

Here's what you do:

1. Visit *www.facthound.com*
2. Choose your grade level.
3. Begin your search.

This book's ID number is 9781429623209.

FactHound will fetch the best sites for you!

Index

FEB '09

SOMERSET NEWJUV
32040001774973
Kortenkamp, Steve.
Space travelers /

DATE DUE